CELEBRATING THE CITY OF LISBON

Celebrating the City of Lisbon

Walter the Educator

Silent King Books

SILENT KING BOOKS

SKB

Copyright © 2024 by Walter the Educator

All rights reserved. No part of this book may be reproduced in any manner whatsoever without written permission except in the case of brief quotations embodied in critical articles and reviews.

First Printing, 2024

Disclaimer
This book is a literary work; the story is not about specific persons, locations, situations, and/or circumstances unless mentioned in a historical context. Any resemblance to real persons, locations, situations, and/or circumstances is coincidental. This book is for entertainment and informational purposes only. The author and publisher offer this information without warranties expressed or implied. No matter the grounds, neither the author nor the publisher will be accountable for any losses, injuries, or other damages caused by the reader's use of this book. The use of this book acknowledges an understanding and acceptance of this disclaimer.

Celebrating the City of Lisbon is a little collectible souvenir book that belongs to the Celebrating Cities Book Series by Walter the Educator. Collect them all and more books at WaltertheEducator.com

USE THE EXTRA SPACE TO TAKE NOTES AND DOCUMENT YOUR MEMORIES

LISBON

In Lisbon's embrace, where the sun kisses the sea,

Celebrating the City of
Lisbon

A tapestry woven with tales of history,

Golden streets bask in a mellow light,

Whispering secrets of day and night.

Through Alfama's labyrinthine ways,

Echoes of fado, ancient and gray,

Saudade lingers in every corner,

A melancholic song, a timeless mourner.

Cobblestones glisten with stories untold,

Each step a memory, a whisper of old,

Celebrating the City of Lisbon

Where trams clatter with nostalgic charm,

Past tiles of azulejos, hand-painted art.

Lisbon's heart beats to the Tagus' song,

A river of dreams, flowing ever strong,

Reflecting bridges like strings of a lyre,

Connecting past and present in a sapphire fire.

On Belém's shores, where explorers once roamed,

The winds still carry tales of the unknown,

Celebrating the City of
Lisbon

From Vasco da Gama to distant lands,

Their courage immortal, in marble stands.

Pastel de nata, a sweet delight,

A symphony of flavors, in the soft twilight,

Cafés hum with laughter, stories unfurled,

In the warmth of Lisbon, a connected world.

The city's pulse quickens in Bairro Alto's night,

Lanterns flicker with a vibrant light,

Music and voices merge in a dance,

A celebration of life, a timeless trance.

From Castelo de São Jorge, the vista wide,

Red rooftops tumble to the riverside,

A patchwork of beauty, in terracotta hues,

A living canvas, ever-changing views.

Under the Ponte 25 de Abril's span,

The city moves with a subtle plan,

Beneath its arches, the future unfolds,

Celebrating the City of
Lisbon

In the spirit of Lisbon, brave and bold.

Gardens of Estrela bloom in serene grace,

A verdant haven, a peaceful space,

Where jacarandas paint the skies with blue,

And time moves gently, like morning dew.

Celebrating the City of
Lisbon

ABOUT THE CREATOR

Walter the Educator is one of the pseudonyms for Walter Anderson. Formally educated in Chemistry, Business, and Education, he is an educator, an author, a diverse entrepreneur, and he is the son of a disabled war veteran. "Walter the Educator" shares his time between educating and creating. He holds interests and owns several creative projects that entertain, enlighten, enhance, and educate, hoping to inspire and motivate you. Follow, find new works, and stay up to date with Walter the Educator™ at

www.ingramcontent.com/pod-product-compliance
Lightning Source LLC
LaVergne TN
LVHW012050070526
838201LV00082B/3900